Inspiration

Remembering Who You Are Journal

Beth Lord

Beth Lord

ISBN-10:1-62269-012-5
ISBN-13:978-1-62269-012-1

Other Books by Beth Lord

Points of Consciousness from The Camino

Finding Otis

The House On 16th Ave. N.E.

La Dolce Vita a Villa Picalò/Living The Sweet Life At Villa Picalò

ASMR:Autonomous Sensory Meridian Response

Five Easy Steps For Turning Your Stories Into Books

Star Essence Journal

A Playbook Between The Memory Challenged Client & The Caregiver

DEDICATION

To You.

I know you in my heart even though I've lost you in the
physical form of how I once knew you.
You are so special to me.
It hurts to remember that you have gone from your body,
but the thoughts and stories you've left behind inspires me.
You inspire me.
There are so many feelings that make me think of you.
I laugh. I cry.
I remember the gift of you.
You have been a gift to me.

I want to pull this journal out when I want to be inspired
by you.

Thank-you for your love.
Thank-you for your spirit and soul.
Thank-you for being you.

"It is a curious thing, the death of a loved one. We all know that our time in this world is limited, and that eventually all of us will end up underneath some sheet, never to wake up. And yet it is always a surprise when it happens to someone we know. It is like walking up the stairs to your bedroom in the dark, and thinking there is one more stair than there is. Your foot falls down, through the air, and there is a sickly moment of dark surprise as you try and readjust the way you thought of things."

— Lemony Snicket, Horseradish

CONTENTS

Acknowledgements		vii
Chapter One	Word Clues	11
Chapter Two	Storylines	19
Chapter Two	Stories That Move Me	41
Chapter Three	Moments That Strike Me	77
Chapter Four	Other Memories	105

"That was the thing. You never got used to it, the idea of someone being gone. Just when you think it's reconciled, accepted, someone points it out to you, and it just hits you all over again, that shocking."

— Sarah Dessen, The Truth About Forever

ACKNOWLEDGMENTS

To Christopher Togawa
Who gave me a deadline to get this done for his friend.
God Bless!

"Death leaves a heartache no one can heal, love leaves a memory no one can steal.

From an Irish headstone"

— Richard Puz, The Carolinian

If writing is difficult for you, record your thoughts and information on a recorder, iPhone, iPad or smart phone, so you play your thoughts back to yourself. These expressed thoughts and conversations are the bridge builders between you and your loved one.

You are collecting your loved one in this journal. We can always turn this journal into a keepsake book for you so let this journal be a guide into your heart. These memories are your inspiration for the rest of your life.

"Whoever said that loss gets easier with time was a liar. Here's what really happens: The spaces between the times you miss them grow longer. Then, when you do remember to miss them again, it's still with a stabbing pain to the heart. And you have guilt. Guilt because it's been too long since you missed them last."

— Kristin O'Donnell Tubb, The 13th Sign

"Death ends a life, not a relationship."
— Mitch Albom, Tuesdays with Morrie

Chapter One

Word Clues

The time to remember their words is now because we quickly forget their spoken words, phrases, and mannerisms. Taking the time to recall these word clues is mapping out the course of this journal for you with stories, adventures, laughter, good times and what they taught you.

"I am always saddened by the death of a good person. It is from this sadness that a feeling of gratitude emerges. I feel honored to have known them and blessed that their passing serves as a reminder to me that my time on this beautiful earth is limited and that I should seize the opportunity I have to forgive, share, explore, and love. I can think of no greater way to honor the deceased than to live this way."

— Steve Maraboli

You can write in this journal alone or invite others to help you remember.
Watch videos of your loved one.
Look at photographs.
Sift through the emails they have sent you.
Cards.
Tape recordings.

Where are the clues?
The Word clues.

"People in the real world always say, when something terrible happens, that the sadness and loss and aching pain of the heart will "lessen as time passes," but it isn't true. Sorrow and loss are constant, but if we all had to go through our whole lives carrying them the whole time, we wouldn't be able to stand it. The sadness would paralyze us. So in the end we just pack it into bags and find somewhere to leave it."

— Fredrik Backman, My Grandmother Asked Me
   to Tell You She's Sorry

Key Words

_____

_____

_____

_____

_____

_____

_____

_____

_____

_____

_____

_____

_____

_____

_____

_____

_____

_____

_____

_____

Key Words

_____

_____

_____

_____

_____

_____

_____

_____

_____

_____

_____

_____

_____

_____

_____

_____

_____

_____

Key Words

_____

_____

_____

_____

_____

_____

_____

_____

_____

_____

_____

_____

_____

_____

_____

_____

_____

_____

_____

Key Words

_____

_____

_____

_____

_____

_____

_____

_____

_____

_____

_____

_____

_____

_____

_____

_____

_____

Chapter Two

StoryLine

"There is no greater agony than bearing an untold story inside you."

— Maya Angelou, I Know Why the Caged Bird Sings

"After nourishment, shelter and companionship, stories are the thing we need most in the world."

— Philip Pullman

The words you wrote down in the first chapter are now turning into a storyline connecting you further into that particular story of your loved one. This storyline is a thread - a simple one to two sentences that connects you to the fullness of the story you are writing about in the next chapter. A storyline is a plot. For example, if one of your words is laughter, your storyline could go something like:

The time Frank managed to get the kids laughing while we had a flat tire in our car and missed our flight to Disney World.

You can also combine words if they bring up a particular story for you. Whatever helps you remember the stories.

"But there's a story behind everything. How a picture got on a wall. How a scar got on your face. Sometimes the stories are simple, and sometimes they are hard and heartbreaking. But behind all your stories is always your mother's story, because hers is where yours begin."

— Mitch Albom, For One More Day

Storyline One:

_____

_____

_____

_____

_____

_____

Storyline Two:

_____

_____

_____

_____

_____

_____

Storyline Three:

_____

_____

_____

_____

_____

_____

Storyline Four:

_____

_____

_____

_____

_____

_____

Storyline Five:

_____

_____

_____

_____

_____

_____

Storyline Six:

_____

_____

_____

_____

_____

_____

Storyline Seven:

_____

_____

_____

_____

_____

_____

Storyline Eight:

_____

_____

_____

_____

_____

_____

Storyline Nine:

_____

_____

_____

_____

_____

_____

Storyline Ten:

_____

_____

_____

_____

_____

_____

Storyline Eleven:

_____

_____

_____

_____

_____

_____

Storyline Twelve:

_____

_____

_____

_____

_____

_____

Storyline Thirteen:

_____

_____

_____

_____

_____

_____

Storyline Fourteen:

_____

_____

_____

_____

_____

_____

Storyline Fifteen:

_____

_____

_____

_____

_____

_____

Storyline Sixteen:

_____

_____

_____

_____

_____

_____

Storyline Seventeen:

_____

_____

_____

_____

_____

_____

_____

Storyline Eighteen:

_____

_____

_____

_____

_____

_____

Storyline Nineteen:

_____

_____

_____

_____

_____

_____

Storyline Twenty:

_____

_____

_____

_____

_____

_____

Storyline Twenty-One:

_____

_____

_____

_____

_____

_____

Storyline Twenty-Two:

_____

_____

_____

_____

_____

_____

Storyline Twenty-Three:

_____

_____

_____

_____

_____

_____

Storyline Twenty-Four:

_____

_____

_____

_____

_____

_____

Storyline Twenty-Five:

_____

_____

_____

_____

_____

_____

Storyline Twenty-Six:

_____

_____

_____

_____

_____

_____

Storyline Twenty-Seven:

_____

_____

_____

_____

_____

_____

Storyline Twenty-eight:

_____

_____

_____

_____

_____

_____

Storyline Twenty-nine:

_____

_____

_____

_____

_____

_____

Storyline Thirty:

_____

_____

_____

_____

_____

_____

Storyline Thirty-One:

_____

_____

_____

_____

_____

_____

_____

Storyline Thirty-Two:

_____

_____

_____

_____

_____

_____

_____

Storyline Thirty-Three:

_____

_____

_____

_____

_____

_____

Storyline Thirty-Four:

_____

_____

_____

_____

_____

Storyline Thirty-Five:

_____

_____

_____

_____

_____

_____

_____

Storyline Thirty-Six:

_____

_____

_____

_____

_____

_____

_____

Chapter Three

The Stories That Move Me

Build on the storylines.

Stories That Move Me

Story One:

_____

_____

_____

_____

_____

_____

_____

_____

_____

_____

_____

_____

_____

_____

_____

_____

Stories That Move Me

Story Two:

_____

_____

_____

_____

_____

_____

_____

_____

_____

_____

_____

_____

_____

_____

_____

_____

_____

_____

Stories That Move Me

Story Three:

_____

_____

_____

_____

_____

_____

_____

_____

_____

_____

_____

_____

_____

_____

_____

_____

_____

_____

Stories That Move Me

Story Four:

_____

_____

_____

_____

_____

_____

_____

_____

_____

_____

_____

_____

_____

_____

_____

_____

_____

Stories That Move Me

Story Five:

_____

_____

_____

_____

_____

_____

_____

_____

_____

_____

_____

_____

_____

_____

_____

_____

_____

_____

Stories That Move Me

Story Six:

_____

_____

_____

_____

_____

_____

_____

_____

_____

_____

_____

_____

_____

_____

_____

_____

_____

_____

Stories That Move Me

Story Seven:

_____

_____

_____

_____

_____

_____

_____

_____

_____

_____

_____

_____

_____

_____

_____

_____

_____

_____

Stories That Move Me

Story Eight:

_____

_____

_____

_____

_____

_____

_____

_____

_____

_____

_____

_____

_____

_____

_____

_____

_____

_____

_____

Stories That Move Me

Story Nine:

_____

_____

_____

_____

_____

_____

_____

_____

_____

_____

_____

_____

_____

_____

_____

_____

Stories That Move Me

Story Ten:

_____

_____

_____

_____

_____

_____

_____

_____

_____

_____

_____

_____

_____

_____

_____

Stories That Move Me

Story Eleven:

_____

_____

_____

_____

_____

_____

_____

_____

_____

_____

_____

_____

_____

_____

_____

_____

_____

Stories That Move Me

Story Twelve:

_____

_____

_____

_____

_____

_____

_____

_____

_____

_____

_____

_____

_____

_____

_____

_____

_____

_____

Stories That Move Me

Story Thirteen:

Stories That Move Me

Story Fourteen:

_____

_____

_____

_____

_____

_____

_____

_____

_____

_____

_____

_____

_____

_____

_____

_____

_____

_____

_____

_____

Stories That Move Me

Story Fifteen:

_____

_____

_____

_____

_____

_____

_____

_____

_____

_____

_____

_____

_____

_____

_____

_____

Stories That Move Me

Story Sixteen:

_____

_____

_____

_____

_____

_____

_____

_____

_____

_____

_____

_____

_____

_____

_____

_____

_____

_____

Stories That Move Me

Story Seventeen:

_____

_____

_____

_____

_____

_____

_____

_____

_____

_____

_____

_____

_____

_____

_____

_____

_____

_____

Stories That Move Me

Story Eighteen:

_____

_____

_____

_____

_____

_____

_____

_____

_____

_____

_____

_____

_____

_____

_____

_____

_____

Stories That Move Me

Story Nineteen:

_____

_____

_____

_____

_____

_____

_____

_____

_____

_____

_____

_____

_____

_____

_____

_____

_____

_____

Stories That Move Me

Story Twenty:

_____

_____

_____

_____

_____

_____

_____

_____

_____

_____

_____

_____

_____

_____

_____

_____

_____

_____

_____

Stories That Move Me

Story Twenty-One:

_____

_____

_____

_____

_____

_____

_____

_____

_____

_____

_____

_____

_____

_____

_____

_____

Stories That Move Me

Story Twenty-Two:

_____

_____

_____

_____

_____

_____

_____

_____

_____

_____

_____

_____

_____

_____

_____

_____

_____

Stories That Move Me

Story Twenty-Three:

_____

_____

_____

_____

_____

_____

_____

_____

_____

_____

_____

_____

_____

_____

_____

_____

_____

_____

_____

Stories That Move Me

Story Twenty-Four:

_____

_____

_____

_____

_____

_____

_____

_____

_____

_____

_____

_____

_____

_____

_____

_____

_____

Stories That Move Me

Story Twenty-Five:

_____

_____

_____

_____

_____

_____

_____

_____

_____

_____

_____

_____

_____

_____

_____

_____

_____

_____

Stories That Move Me

Story Twenty-Six:

_____

_____

_____

_____

_____

_____

_____

_____

_____

_____

_____

_____

_____

_____

_____

_____

_____

_____

_____

Stories That Move Me

Story Twenty-Seven:

_____

_____

_____

_____

_____

_____

_____

_____

_____

_____

_____

_____

_____

_____

_____

_____

_____

Stories That Move Me

Story Twenty-Eight:

_____

_____

_____

_____

_____

_____

_____

_____

_____

_____

_____

_____

_____

_____

_____

_____

_____

_____

Stories That Move Me

Story Twenty-Nine:

_____

_____

_____

_____

_____

_____

_____

_____

_____

_____

_____

_____

_____

_____

_____

_____

_____

_____

Stories That Move Me

Story Thirty:

_____

_____

_____

_____

_____

_____

_____

_____

_____

_____

_____

_____

_____

_____

_____

_____

_____

_____

_____

Stories That Move Me

Story Thirty-One:

_____

_____

_____

_____

_____

_____

_____

_____

_____

_____

_____

_____

_____

_____

_____

Stories That Move Me

Story Thirty-Two:

_____

_____

_____

_____

_____

_____

_____

_____

_____

_____

_____

_____

_____

_____

_____

_____

_____

_____

Stories That Move Me

Story Thirty-Three:

_____

_____

_____

_____

_____

_____

_____

_____

_____

_____

_____

_____

_____

_____

_____

_____

_____

Stories That Move Me

Story Thirty-Four:

_____

_____

_____

_____

_____

_____

_____

_____

_____

_____

_____

_____

_____

_____

_____

_____

_____

Stories That Move Me

Story Thirty-Five:

Chapter Three

Moments That Strike Me

We forget. We go on about our life, but we hold on to memories, items and anything that brings us back to this person. So this chapter is all about these times.

What is it that is going to bring you back to this person?

It's ok to know that this pain and grief are going to be inside of you. They are part of the love you have for this person. The meaning around your life has changed. It's ok. Hold on to this person for dear life if it helps you remember this love.

"Will. For a moment her heart hesitated. She remembered when Will had died, her agony, the long nights alone, reaching across the bed every morning when she woke up, for years expecting to find him there, and only slowly growing accustomed to the fact that side of the bed would always be empty. The moments when she had found something funny and turned to share the joke with him, only to be shocked anew that he was not there. The worst moments, when, sitting alone at breakfast, she had realized that she had forgotten the precise blue of his eyes or the depth of his laugh; that, like the sound of Jem's violin music, they had faded into the distance where memories are silent."

— Cassandra Clare, Clockwork Princess

Moments That Strike Me

_____

_____

_____

_____

_____

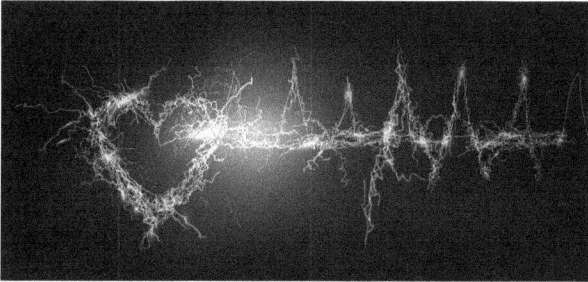

Moments That Strike Me

_____

_____

_____

_____

_____

Moments That Strike Me

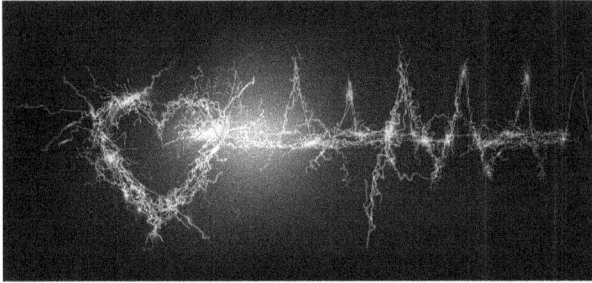

Moments That Strike Me

Moments That Strike Me

_____

_____

_____

_____

_____

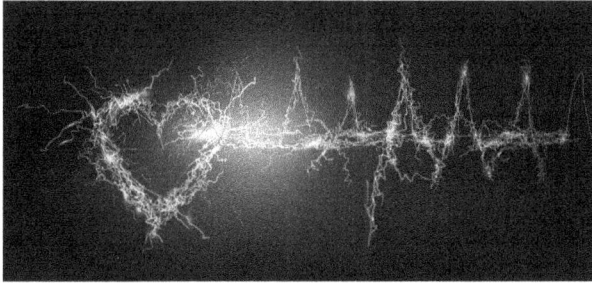

Moments That Strike Me

_____

_____

_____

_____

_____

Moments That Strike Me

_____

_____

_____

_____

_____

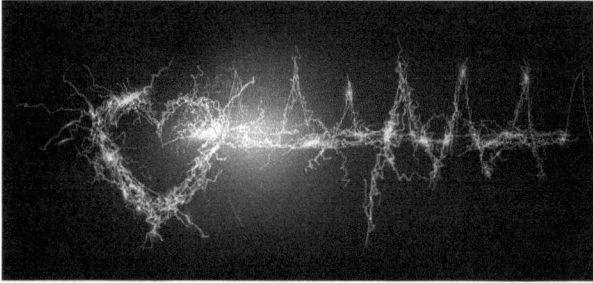

Moments That Strike Me

_____

_____

_____

_____

_____

Moments That Strike Me

_____

_____

_____

_____

_____

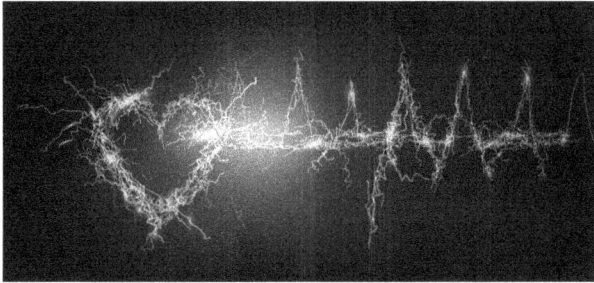

Moments That Strike Me

_____

_____

_____

_____

_____

Moments That Strike Me

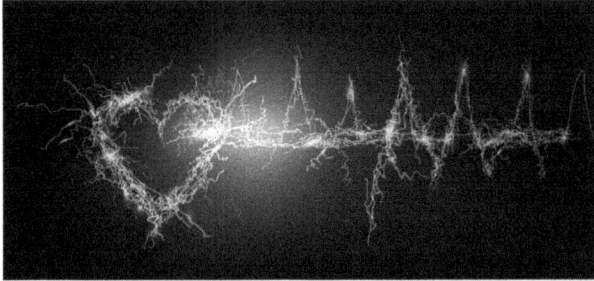

Moments That Strike Me

Moments That Strike Me

_____

_____

_____

_____

_____

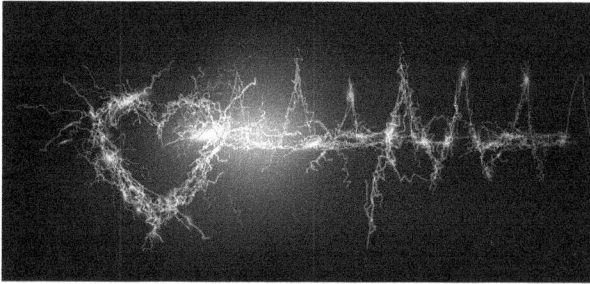

Moments That Strike Me

_____

_____

_____

_____

Moments That Strike Me

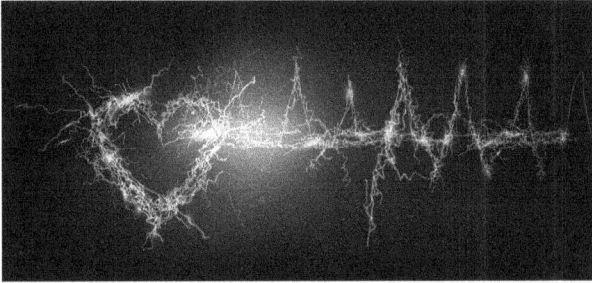

Moments That Strike Me

Moments That Strike Me

_____

_____

_____

_____

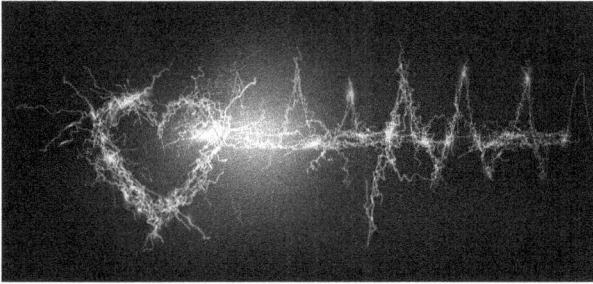

Moments That Strike Me

_____

_____

_____

_____

Moments That Strike Me

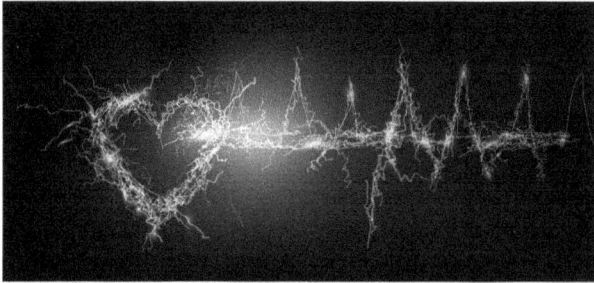

Moments That Strike Me

Moments That Strike Me

_____

_____

_____

_____

_____

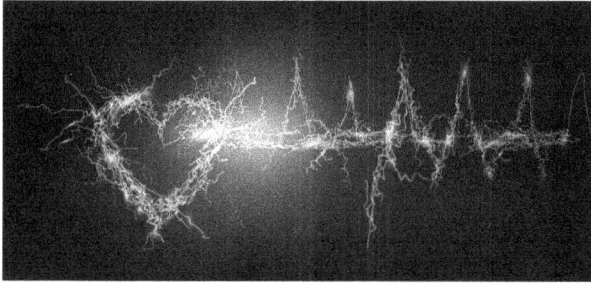

Moments That Strike Me

_____

_____

_____

_____

_____

Moments That Strike Me

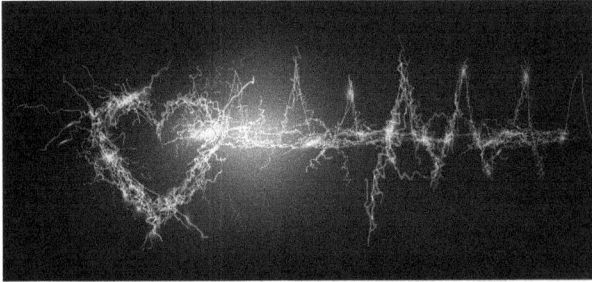

Moments That Strike Me

Moments That Strike Me

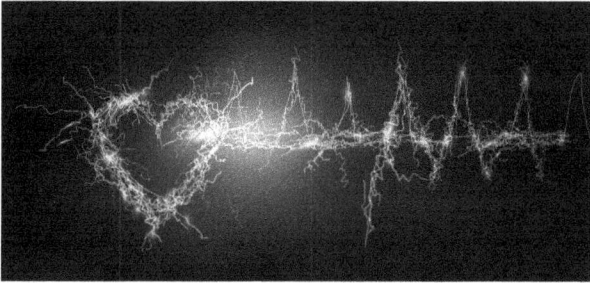

Moments That Strike Me

Moments That Strike Me

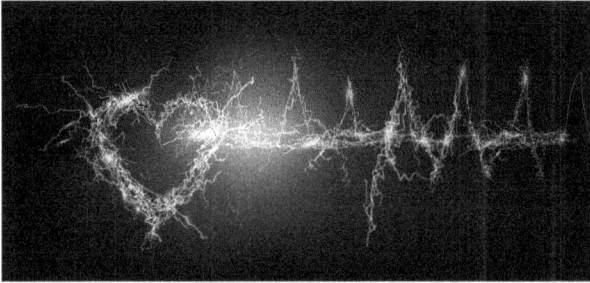

Moments That Strike Me

Moments That Strike Me

_____

_____

_____

_____

_____

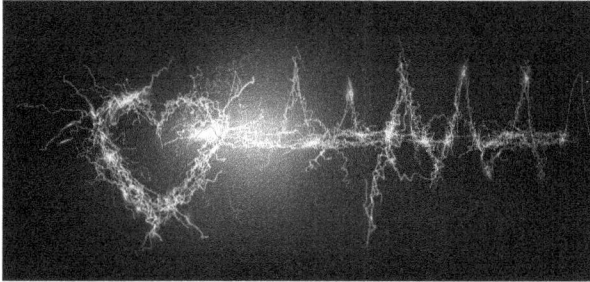

Moments That Strike Me

_____

_____

_____

_____

_____

Moments That Strike Me

_____

_____

_____

_____

_____

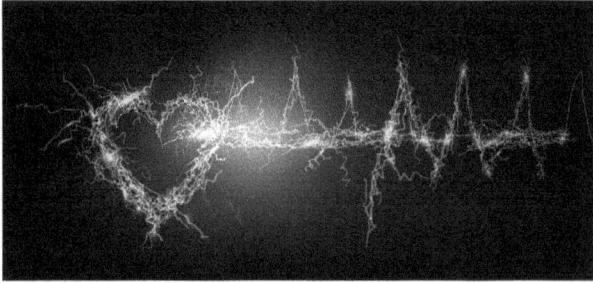

Moments That Strike Me

_____

_____

_____

_____

_____

Moments That Strike Me

_____

_____

_____

_____

_____

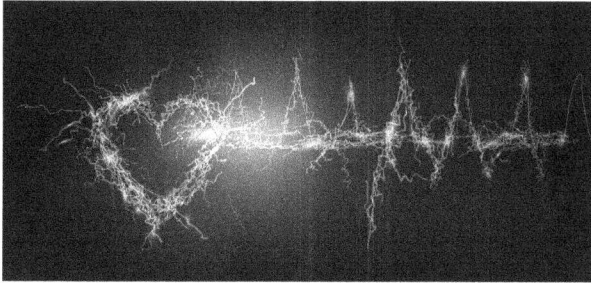

Moments That Strike Me

_____

_____

_____

_____

_____

Moments That Strike Me

_____

_____

_____

_____

_____

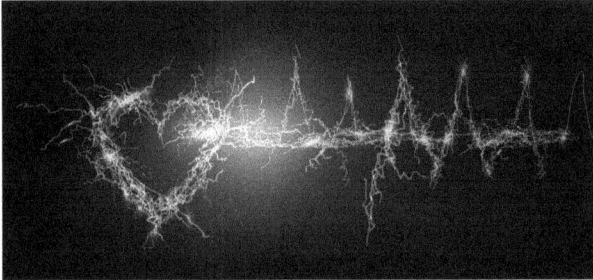

Moments That Strike Me

_____

_____

_____

_____

_____

Moments That Strike Me

_____

_____

_____

_____

_____

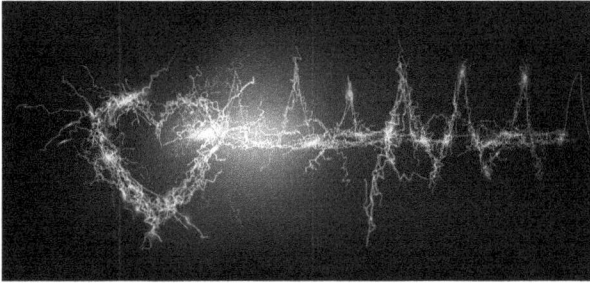

Moments That Strike Me

_____

_____

_____

_____

_____

Moments That Strike Me

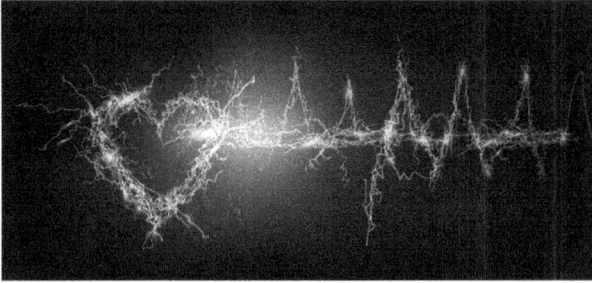

Moments That Strike Me

Moments That Strike Me

_____

_____

_____

_____

_____

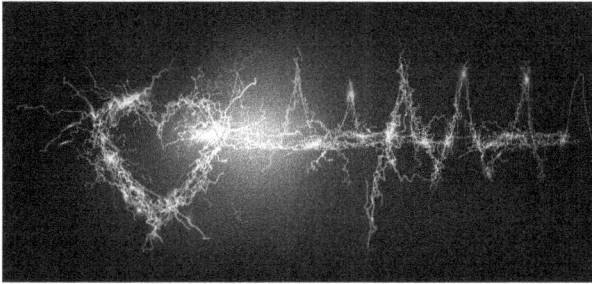

Moments That Strike Me

_____

_____

_____

_____

_____

Moments That Strike Me

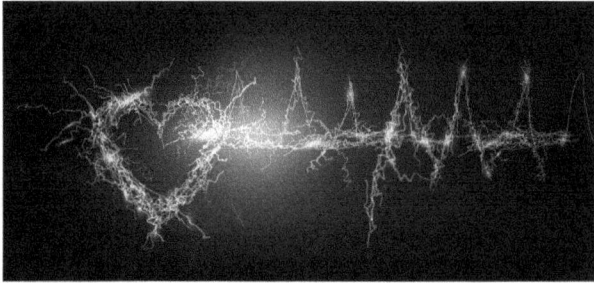

Moments That Strike Me

Moments That Strike Me

_____

_____

_____

_____

_____

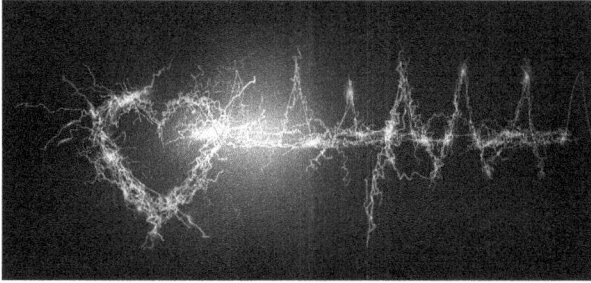

Moments That Strike Me

_____

_____

_____

_____

_____

Moments That Strike Me

_____

_____

_____

_____

_____

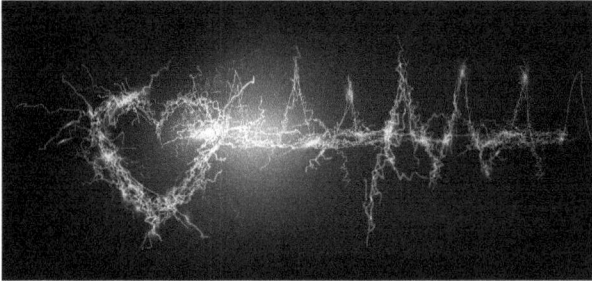

Moments That Strike Me

_____

_____

_____

_____

_____

Moments That Strike Me

_____

_____

_____

_____

_____

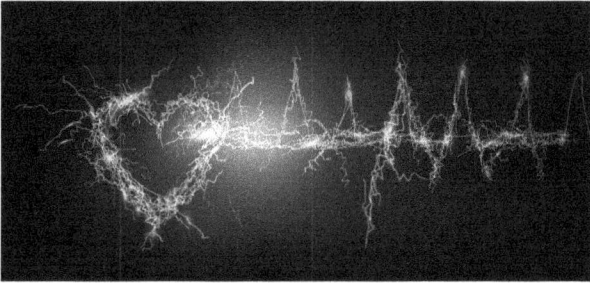

Moments That Strike Me

_____

_____

_____

_____

_____

Moments That Strike Me

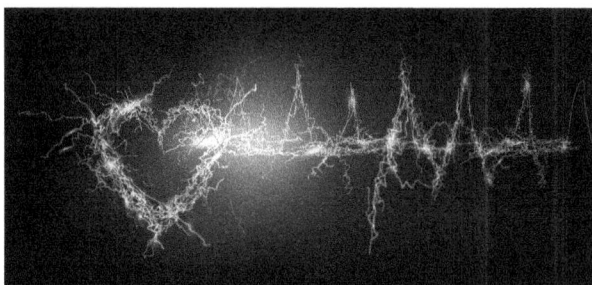

Moments That Strike Me

Chapter Four

Your Thoughts & Other Memories

Your Thoughts & Other Memories

Your Thoughts & Other Memories

Your Thoughts & Other Memories

Your Thoughts & Other Memories

Your Thoughts & Other Memories

Your Thoughts & Other Memories

Your Thoughts & Other Memories

Your Thoughts & Other Memories

Your Thoughts & Other Memories

Your Thoughts & Other Memories

Your Thoughts & Other Memories

Your Thoughts & Other Memories

Your Thoughts & Other Memories

.

Your Thoughts & Other Memories

Your Thoughts & Other Memories

Your Thoughts & Other Memories

Your Thoughts & Other Memories

Your Thoughts & Other Memories

Your Thoughts & Other Memories

Your Thoughts & Other Memories

Your Thoughts & Other Memories

Your Thoughts & Other Memories

Your Thoughts & Other Memories

ABOUT THE AUTHOR

Beth Lord

Beth Lord is a writer and a therapist who combines her passion and knowledge to fulfill her calling to help those in need to share a story with the world. She owns Beth Lord's Write Heart Memories®, where she turns your stories into books. She's been an Occupational Therapist, Feldenkrais Practitioner and a Corporate Sales Representative in the Pharmaceutical Industry.

To find out more about Beth Lord and her work, visit her web page http://www.bethlord.com/

"We're all stories, in the end."
— Steven Moffat

www.ingramcontent.com/pod-product-compliance
Lightning Source LLC
Chambersburg PA
CBHW071557040426
42452CB00008B/1203